Design: Niels Bonnemeier
Production: Patty Holden
Translator: Christie Tam
Editors: Monika Römer, Gabriele Heßmann, Lisa M. Tooker
Food Editor: Rosemary Mark
©2003 Verlag W. Hölker GmbH, Münster
English translation for the U.S. market ©2006 Silverback Books, Inc.
ISBN: 1-59637-073-4
Printed in China

Angelika Ilies

Little

Coffee Book

Contents

Unless otherwise indicated, all recipes make four servings.

Introduction

Whether coffee is used as a morning wakeup or a mid-day stimulant, whether you drink it with lunch or as an afternoon pick-me-up, coffee is our favorite beverage! People drink an average of 3–4 cups a day. Of course, this means that many people drink much more than that, since statistics also take into account every child and tea drinker.

A lot has changed in the past century, including coffee. Our great-grandmothers were still very involved in its preparation: The beans were freshly ground, not too fine and not too coarse, and—of course—using a little elbow grease. For each cup, they placed one heaping spoonful of ground coffee in a carefully preheated coffee pot, poured in boiling water and let the mixture brew under a heavy coffee cozy for 5–7 minutes.

Our grandmothers had an easier time of it: Electric coffee grinders now took over the job of grinding and the invention of the coffee filter revolutionized brewing. For our mothers, making coffee was further simplified. They could buy coffee already ground and every household was equipped with its own coffeemaker to take over the task. A cup of filter coffee was available at all times.

Today, coffee is available in an almost infinite variety of incarnations. Whether instant coffee or traditional filter coffee, Italian espresso or Turkish or Greek mocha, café au lait, melange or cappuccino, iced coffee or vanilla-flavored, there's something for everyone, and there's always something new. But one thing has stayed the same: The incomparable pleasure that coffee brings. As a hot or cold beverage in an endless number of new variations, served with pastry or a hearty treat, or as a sophisticated seasoning in cakes and desserts—let this little book be your guide on a journey of discovery through the world of coffee.

Brief History of Coffee

Where did coffee come from? When and how was this black pick-me-up created? Unfortunately, no one knows for sure; there are no concrete facts. According to one story, however, shepherds in Abyssinia (present-day Ethiopia) were mystified by the strange behavior of their goats. Whenever the animals ate the fruit of a certain plant, they wouldn't be able to fall asleep. Bothered by this, the shepherds brought some of the red cherry-like fruit to a nearby monastery. The monks believed the devil was behind this and threw the berries into the fire. A wonderful fragrance was released but the seeds and fruit were not burned up. The monks finally used these berries to prepare an infusion, drank it and were themselves kept wide awake all night long.

One thing that we do know for sure is that the first coffee plants actually did grow in Abyssinia and that coffee was already considered a beverage in Arabia by the mid-15th century. The Arabs at that time called it "qahwah," which basically means "wine," referring to coffee's intoxicating effect.

In the second half of the 15th century, the coffee bean conquered the Arabian empire by way of Mecca and Medina. The practice of drinking this new beverage was probably spread above all by the pilgrims visiting the shrine in Mecca. They were forbidden to drink alcohol, which made the effects of coffee all the more welcome. Coffee bars came into being, but were then temporarily banned in 1511.

Nevertheless, coffee's triumphal march could not be halted and this black beverage quickly spread to all corners of Arabia. Coffee houses where people were able to enjoy the beverage sprang up everywhere. Soon afterwards, in 1554, the first coffee house on European soil was opened in Constantinople (now Istanbul) and, barely 100 years after that, a second opened on St. Mark's Square in Venice. Over the next few years and centuries, coffee houses continued to proliferate in Europe, including London, Vienna and Paris.

Until the 16th century, the Arabs allowed only roasted beans to be shipped across the seas. The most important port of export was the city of Mocha (in Yemen) on the Red Sea. The export of coffee plants or viable coffee beans was strictly forbidden and subject to harsh penalties. The sultan wanted coffee to remain a secret of the Ottomans. Obviously, this couldn't be managed indefinitely and in the early 17th century, the first seeds of the coffee plant were finally smuggled out of the country. The systematic cultivation of fruit-bearing plants began immediately; there was a high demand in European countries. The monopoly had been broken and the rapid spread of this profitable plant could no longer be stopped. The colonial powers gradually introduced it to all the regions suitable for its cultivation and, of course, to their homelands and the peoples of Europe.

Important: Varieties, Not Brands

People generally buy familiar brands of coffee with nice-sounding names. Few customers choose their beans or ground coffee on the basis of the variety of the coffee itself, and usually only in special shops. Conventional coffee brands are almost always a mixture of various coffee varieties that may even come from several different regions of cultivation in different parts of the world. Almost all coffee is derived from two major coffee varieties: "Arabica" and "robusta."

The first coffee plants in Ethiopia were of the "arabica" variety, which was already being systematically cultivated in Yemen in the 15th century. "Robusta," the second largest coffee variety, was first discovered in Africa in 1898, and the first plantations to grow robusta were introduced on Java in 1900. Today, robusta makes up about 30 percent of world production.

Arabica coffee is considered especially fine and valuable. It is aromatic, mild and low in acidity and low on caffeine. Robusta, on the other hand—as the name implies—is less susceptible to climatic changes and is more disease-resistant, hardier and correspondingly less expensive. At the same time, robusta contains much more caffeine and is stronger, but is also more bitter, more acidic and less aromatic.

The coffee variety isn't the only factor affecting the final quality of coffee. The origin of the beans is just as important. Where were they grown? At what altitude and in what type of soil? How was the climate? Another major factor is the method and intensity of roasting, as well as the ratio of different coffee varieties in the mix.

But, ultimately, it's a matter of personal taste. So the best thing to do is to gradually try a number of different types of coffee until you discover your favorites.

From the Tree to the Bean

The coffee tree thrives only in a tropical climate and is cultivated in many countries. It takes two or three years before a tree produces its first fruits which, when fully ripe, are bright red and resemble small cherries. Traditionally, only the ripe coffee cherries are picked. Because both flowers and cherries at all stages of ripeness are present on the tree simultaneously, harvesting is understandably complex. Often ripe and unripe cherries are stripped from the tree together and sorted afterward.

After picking and sorting, the beans (= two seeds) are extracted from the cherries. The beans are fermented for up to two days and then washed to loosen the sticky pulp. Still enclosed in their seed coats (a protective parchment covering), they are finally dried either in the sun or in hot-air dryers. Just before export, this protective covering is also removed. Coffee handlers from all over the world buy the greenish-gray "raw coffee," sort the beans and then roast them. Today, roasting is performed in large roasters at about 400°F and takes only a few minutes. During the process, the beans double in size, the roasted and bitter components are created and essential oils are released. After roasting, the beans are rapidly cooled, mixed with other varieties of coffee beans and packaged immediately. Speed is required after roasting to keep the precious aroma from dissipating.

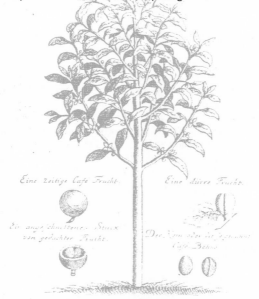

Eine zeitige Cafe Frucht.

Eine dürre Frucht.

Ein angeschnittener Strauk
von gedachter Frucht.

Der Kern oder die gegrannte
Cafe Bonne.

Coffee Houses

As mentioned above, the first coffee houses were established as early as the 15th century. They served as both a meeting place and a news center, a stage and a foyer, a place of quiet and of excitement. Here people could relax and exchange news of recent events, forge political alliances or hear the latest gossip. This was equally the case in Istanbul, Venice, Vienna, London, and even New York where, according to legend, the first coffee house was opened on American soil in 1658. There are now many different types of coffee houses all over the world; coffee lovers can enjoy an authentic "melange" in a Viennese Kaffeehaus, down a quick "espresso" in a bar on a market square, or get an iced coffee to go in a typical American coffee shop and take it to a nearby park.

Recently, coffee has conquered the world all over again, this time in the form of the "coffee shop" from the United States. It used to be that these shops (usually identified by neon signs) were open only for breakfast; now they've become stylish locales enticing patrons until late into the evening. Once it was common practice simply to pour hot water over a few spoonfuls of instant coffee and provide the traditional—and tasteless—infinite refills, but today's beverage menus are expected to include espresso, cappuccino, iced coffee and various other innovative new coffee creations. For instance, how about a coffee flavored with mint syrup?

In many countries throughout the world, these

coffee shops are all the rage. People meet at the bar for a quick coffee, Italian espresso or French café au lait, or take a break to visit with friends and dine on a sandwich, salad, burger or bagel with, of course, a large coffee—preferably enhanced with the flavoring of their choice.

Fortunately, however, it is still possible to find cozy coffee houses, which continue to serve as ideal places for relaxing with a good cup of coffee, a delicious piece of cake and the day's newspaper.

Coffee, Caffè, Café or Kaffee— International Pick-Me-Up

Brauner • Typically found in the Viennese coffee houses; a black coffee (espresso) with milk or cream.

Café au lait • Essential accompaniment to a fresh croissant. Finely ground coffee is prepared in a filter and combined with hot milk in a typical "bol" (a handleless bowl). Swiss Germans call it a "schale" and serve it in a cup.

Café cortado • A favorite in Spain, café cortado is a small, strong coffee or espresso with a little bit of hot milk served in a small espresso cup or glass.

Caffè corto • Espresso that is brewed very briefly and extremely strong. Similar to a caffè ristretto.

Caffè latte • Italian milk-and-coffee drink comprising espresso and a lot of hot milk. The espresso is poured into a tall glass and then topped with foamed milk.

Caffè ristretto/espresso ristretto • Small, very strong espresso prepared with 2 tablespoons ground espresso coffee and only 2 tablespoons water (traditional espresso uses $1/2$ cup water).

Capo • Coffee with enough milk to turn it dark brown, served in a small demitasse (at least it is in a traditional Viennese coffee house).

Cappuccino • About one-third espresso and two-thirds hot, steamed milk, a specialty enjoyed by Italians at about 10:00 am. Authentic only if topped with a brownish foam created by the espresso's "crema" and not by sprinkling cocoa powder. Sugar is added according to personal preference and stirred in very carefully to preserve the foam.

Carajillo • Spanish coffee with brandy.

Coffee on the rocks • Place 2 ice cubes and about 1–2 tablespoons sugar in a whiskey glass and add hot espresso.

Decaffeinated coffee • Coffee from which the caffeine has been extracted by means of steam or solvents. May contain no more than 0.1 percent caffeine.

Einspänner • Small, strong espresso topped with a thick layer of sweetened whipped cream, authentically served in a tall, heavy glass mug.

Espresso • Strong and typically Italian. The further south in Italy, the stronger and smaller the espresso. It is genuine only if the deep black coloring is crowned by the "crema," a delicate, medium-brown foam topping. However, this is possible only with the aid of the right ground coffee and a good machine. Espresso coffee beans are an especially strong and dark roast and the espresso machine must force the water through the grounds at high pressure and lightning speed. A large part of the coffee's stimulant effect is then eliminated in the process, making espresso easier to digest than filter coffee.

Espresso con panna • Classic espresso with a small dollop of whipped cream on top.

Espresso corretto • Espresso that has been "corrected" with liqueur or a shot of Grappa or brandy.

Espresso doppio • Double espresso.

Espresso machiatto • "Stained" espresso, i.e. topped with a tiny bit of foamed milk. If you add more milk, it becomes a classic cappuccino.

Espresso romano • Espresso enhanced with a little lime peel. Similar to a Brazilian "cafezinho," a small cup of strong, dark-roast coffee.

Fiaker • An einspänner with a shot of Kirsch, sometimes even with rum or raspberry liqueur.

Flavored coffee • Trendy and only for those who like it—coffee flavored with syrup.

Franziskaner • Coffee with lots of cream, resulting in a light-brown mixture the same color as a Franciscan Monk's robes.

Iced cappuccino • Cappuccino with ice cubes.

Iced coffee • Place ice cubes in a glass and fill halfway with cold coffee. Then add cold milk and stir in sugar and vanilla to taste. If desired, top with whipped cream.

Kaffee creme • Espresso served in a pot with a small pitcher of cream on the side.

Kaffee verkehrt (coffee reversed) • Lots of hot milk and a little filter coffee. A light and digestible beverage. In French-speaking Switzerland, it's also known as a "renversé."

Kapuziner • Strong coffee or espresso with just enough cream to make it the same color as a Capuchin monk's robes. Darker than a "Franziskaner."

Konsul • Black coffee with a little cream.

Latte macchiato • Almost the exact opposite of espresso

Macchiato • Hot steamed milk is poured into a tall glass and freshly brewed espresso poured over the top.

Mocchacino • Espresso with hot milk or hot chocolate topped with foamed milk or whipped cream. Can be prepared in many different ways.

Mocha • Originally a valuable variety of coffee made from small beans grown in the Ethiopian Highlands. These beans were shipped from the Yemeni port of Mocha (located on the Red Sea), which is where they got their name. Today this term usually means black coffee prepared with an espresso machine at a ratio of 2 tablespoons ground coffee to about $1/4$ cup water for a small mocha and 3 tablespoons coffee to 1 cup water for a large mocha. The surface should be covered with a brownish, slightly foamy layer (like the crema on espresso).

Schümli • A Swiss drink. Light-roast coffee beans are freshly ground and brewed one cup at a time under pressure, like espresso. Each cup has a little light foam on top.

Schwarzer • Viennese espresso without milk.

Turkish coffee • A favorite in the Arab-Turkish world, it is prepared in a "cezve," a tall copper, brass or stainless steel pot with a long handle. To make one serving, combine 1 heaping teaspoon light-roast, very finely ground coffee (usually Arabica), the desired amount of sugar and $1/4$ cup water in the cezve. Heat and when the coffee starts to bubble up, remove it from the burner and wait for the foam to settle. Then return it to the burner. Do this up to three times. Then wait briefly for the coffee grounds to settle to the bottom and pour coffee into tiny cups. Depending on the region and individual preferences, Turkish coffee may be seasoned with cardamom, saffron, cloves or cinnamon. The preparation of Greek coffee is modeled after the Turkish tradition.

Verlängerter • Espresso prepared with twice as much water and with cream served on the side.

Viennese Melange • Espresso or strong filter coffee with an equal amount of hot milk and topped with foamed milk.

Coffee Tips

- If possible, drink only fresh coffee.
- Don't keep coffee warm on a burner because it ruins the flavor.
- Do not reheat.
- Buy only small amounts that you can use up quickly.
- If possible, buy only whole beans and grind them as needed.
- When buying ground coffee, be sure to get the correct grind.
- Coarsely ground coffee is intended for brewing in a pot, medium-fine is for use in a filter and extremely fine is suitable for preparing espresso.
- If you don't break the seal on vacuum-packed coffee, it will keep its aroma for several months. Once you open a package, use it up quickly.
- Always keep coffee beans and ground coffee in sealed containers so they won't lose their aroma.
- Keep ground coffee in a cool place, preferably the refrigerator. For longer periods of time, store it in the freezer; this will keep the oils it contains from turning rancid.
- Always drink a glass of water with your coffee. Caffeine flushes water out of your system, which is why drinking coffee always makes you thirsty.

Pastries Typically
Served with Coffee

Cantuccini

1 $^2/_3$ cups almonds, 4 $^1/_4$ cups all-purpose flour,
1 cup sugar, 1 $^1/_2$ teaspoons baking powder,
1 pinch salt, 4 eggs, 1 egg yolk,
Zest and juice from 1 orange, 1 pinch saffron
Plus: Flour for the work surface,
1 egg yolk for brushing on

In an ungreased pan, toast almonds lightly and let cool.

In a bowl, combine flour, sugar, baking powder and salt. Add eggs, egg yolk and orange zest. Stir in saffron and 1 tablespoon orange juice. Knead together to form a smooth dough. Cover and let stand for 30 minutes.

Preheat oven to 350°F. Line a baking sheet with parchment paper. Dust your hands with flour and knead almonds into the dough. Shape dough into 2 cylinders (about 1 $^1/_2$ inches thick), press slightly flat and place on the baking sheet.

Whisk together egg yolk and 1 tablespoon water and brush onto the cylinders. Bake in the oven for about 40 minutes until golden-brown, occasionally brushing on remaining orange juice.

Remove cylinders from the oven and cut on an angle into $^1/_2$ inch slices. Arrange slices flat on the baking sheet and brown in the oven for another few minutes.

Amaretti

2 cups powdered sugar, 2 cups blanched ground
almonds, 1 tablespoon all-purpose flour, 1 pinch
cinnamon, 3 egg whites, $\frac{1}{2}$ teaspoon grated
lemon zest, Several drops almond extract

Preheat oven to 350°F. Line 2 baking sheets with
parchment paper. Sift powdered sugar into a bowl and
add almonds, flour and cinnamon. In a second large
bowl, beat egg whites until lightly foamy. Stir in lemon
zest. Gradually stir in almond mixture, then add
almond extract.

Spoon small mounds of batter onto the baking sheets,
making sure to leave adequate spacing in between the
mounds. Bake in the oven on the middle rack for about
15 minutes. Transfer immediately to a cooling rack and
let cool.

Blueberry Muffins

$\frac{1}{2}$ cup softened butter, $\frac{3}{4}$ cup plus 2 tablespoons
sugar, 2 eggs, 1 teaspoon ground vanilla extract,
1 pinch salt, 2 cups flour,
2 teaspoons baking powder, $\frac{2}{3}$ cup buttermilk,
1$\frac{1}{4}$ cups small blueberries (fresh or frozen)
Plus: Butter for the pan

Grease a muffin pan with 12 muffin cups. Beat butter and sugar until smooth. Stir in eggs, vanilla and salt. Combine flour and baking powder and gradually stir into batter, alternating with buttermilk.

Preheat oven to 350°F. Sort blueberries, rinse, pat dry and carefully fold into the batter. If you use frozen berries, fold in without thawing. Spoon batter into muffin cups. Bake in the oven for about 35 minutes.

Buttermilk Scones

2 cups all-purpose flour, ¼ cup sugar,
1½ teaspoons baking powder, ½ teaspoon salt,
¼ cup softened butter, 1 egg, ½ cup buttermilk
Plus: Flour for the work surface

Preheat oven to 400°F. Line a baking sheet with parchment paper. In a bowl, combine flour, sugar, baking powder and salt. Gradually stir in butter, egg and buttermilk. Mix into a very soft dough.

On a well floured work surface, shape dough into a sheet no more than 1 inch thick. Cut out 2½ inch disks and place on a baking sheet, leaving adequate spacing in between. Knead leftover dough, roll out again and cut out more disks.

Bake scones in the oven for 15 to 20 minutes until golden-brown. Best served warm.

Donuts

$^{1}/_{4}$ cup softened butter, 3 eggs, $^{3}/_{4}$ cup sugar,
$^{3}/_{4}$ cup plus 2 tablespoons milk, 1 teaspoon ground
vanilla, 1 pinch salt, 1 pinch freshly grated nutmeg,
5 cups all-purpose flour, 3 teaspoons baking powder
Plus: Flour for the work surface, Oil for frying,
Sugar for coating

Beat butter, eggs and sugar until smooth. Stir in milk,
vanilla, salt and nutmeg. Add flour and baking powder
and gradually work into a dough. On a floured work
surface, roll out dough into a sheet $^{1}/_{2}$ inch thick. Using
a glass, cut out disks about 3 inches across and cut a
$1^{1}/_{4}$ inch disk out of the center of each to form rings.

Heat a large amount of oil to 350°F. Deep-fry donuts
in batches until golden-brown on all sides, reshaping
the hole in the center with the handle of a wooden
spoon as necessary. Remove with a slotted spoon
and drain well on paper towels. Dredge in sugar and
serve immediately.

Chocolate Chip Cookies

²/₃ cup softened butter, 6 tablespoons sugar,
6 tablespoons brown sugar, ¹/₂ teaspoon salt,
¹/₂ teaspoon vanilla, 1 egg, 1¹/₄ cups all-purpose flour,
1 teaspoon baking powder, ²/₃ cup walnuts,
4 ounces chocolate chips or chopped
semisweet chocolate

Preheat oven to 375°F. Line 2 baking sheets with parchment paper. Beat butter, both types of sugar, salt and vanilla until smooth. Stir in egg. Combine flour and baking powder and stir into the dough. Chop walnuts and stir nuts and chocolate chips or chopped chocolate into the dough.

Place 1 tablespoon mounds of dough on the cookie sheets, leaving adequate spacing in between. Bake in the oven for about 10 minutes and then cool on a cooling rack.

Turkish Syrup Balls

1 pound soft goat cheese (chevre), 3 eggs,
2 teaspoons sugar, ½ teaspoon vanilla,
1 dash cinnamon, 1 cup all-purpose flour,
1 teaspoon baking powder
For the syrup: 2½ cups sugar,
Juice from 1 lemon or orange

Preheat oven to 350°F and line 2 baking sheets with parchment paper.

Combine cheese, eggs, sugar, vanilla and cinnamon. Mix flour and baking powder and stir into dough.

Use 2 teaspoons to transfer small mounds of dough to the baking sheets, leaving adequate spacing in between. Bake in the oven for about 20 minutes until golden-brown. Remove and let cool.

For the syrup: In a wide saucepan, combine 2 cups water, sugar and lemon or orange juice and bring to a boil. Reduce over medium heat for about 15 minutes or until syrupy. Let cool slightly.

Pierce balls several times with a toothpick and dredge in syrup. Cover and let stand for at least 30 minutes.

Spanish Churros

The Spanish enjoy this deep-fried choux pastry for breakfast.

2 tablespoons softened butter, 2 tablespoons sugar,
1 pinch salt, 2 cups flour, 2 eggs, Oil for frying,
Powdered sugar for garnish (optional)

In a saucepan, combine 1 cup water, butter, sugar and salt; bring to a boil. Remove from heat. Sift in flour and stir until the batter becomes one big dumpling and pulls away from the bottom of the pan. Using a wooden spoon, work eggs one at a time into the batter.

Heat a large amount of oil to 350°F. Spoon batter into a pastry bag with a large star tip and pipe onto parchment paper in the shape of rings or strips. Place in the hot oil in batches and fry until golden. Remove with a slotted spoon and drain on paper towels. If desired, cut into smaller pieces and dust with powdered sugar.

Croissants

1 package ($^1/_4$ ounce) active dry yeast,
1 cup lukewarm milk (110−120°F), 2 tablespoons
sugar, 4 cups flour, $^1/_2$ teaspoon salt, 2 eggs,
1 cup (2 sticks) softened butter
Plus: Flour for the work surface,
1 egg yolk for brushing on

Combine yeast, milk and $^1/_4$ teaspoon sugar in a small bowl. Let stand for about 15 minutes until foamy.

Add flour, remaining sugar, salt and eggs and knead into soft dough. Cover dough and let stand for about 2 hours at room temperature until it doubles in size.

Punch down dough, cover and refrigerate for at least 3 hours (or overnight).

On the next day, thoroughly knead dough on a floured surface. Roll out into a square (but not too thin) and dust with flour.

Cut the butter into $^1/_3$ inch slices. Place the pieces side-by-side in the center of the dough. Fold the corners of the dough over the butter so it is fully covered and press down lightly.

Once again, roll out dough into a square on a floured surface, being careful not to squeeze out the butter. This requires using even pressure and rolling the dough alternately from back to front and from right to left.

Fold the dough to make three equal-sized layers. Roll out and fold two more times, each time dusting the work surface with sufficient flour and refrigerating the dough for 15 minutes before rolling it out again. Roll out dough to a rectangle of about 12 x 20 inches, then cut in half crosswise to form 2 strips about 6 inches wide. Cut each strip into 6 triangles (for a total of 12). Starting from the longest side, roll up the triangles tightly and bend into crescents. Place on a baking sheet with the corner on the bottom, cover and let rise for 20 minutes.

Preheat oven to 425°F. Brush croissants with whisked egg yolk and bake in the oven for about 15 minutes until golden-brown.

Panettone

Makes 1 springform pan (8 inches diameter)

1 package ($^1/_4$ ounce) active dry yeast, $^2/_3$ cup lukewarm
milk (110–120°F), 1 teaspoon sugar, $3^1/_3$ cups
all-purpose flour, 5 egg yolks, 1 pinch salt,
$^3/_4$ cup ($1^1/_2$ sticks) softened butter, $1^1/_4$ cups dried fruit
(combination of raisins, dates, figs, candied lemon
peel, candied orange peel), $^1/_2$ cup chopped almonds
Plus: Butter for the pan, Flour for the pan, 1 egg yolk
for brushing on, Powdered sugar for garnish

Combine yeast, $^1/_4$ cup milk, sugar and enough flour to
make a wet dough or sponge. Let stand for several
minutes until foamy. In a bowl, combine sponge with
remaining milk, remaining flour, egg yolks, salt and
butter and knead into a smooth dough. Cover and let
rise in a warm place for about 1 hour.

Line the edges of the springform pan with a wide strip
of aluminum foil to form an 8 inch high border around
the edges. Thoroughly grease pan and foil, and dust
with flour.

Finely dice the dried fruit. Knead fruit and almonds
into the dough. Transfer dough to the prepared pan,
cover and let rise for another 30 minutes.

Preheat oven to 400°F. Whisk together egg yolk and
1 tablespoon water and brush onto the cake. Bake on

the bottom rack for about 45 minutes until golden-brown. Let cool in the pan for 20 minutes, then remove carefully, place on a cooling rack, cover with a cloth and let cool completely. Serve dusted with powdered sugar.

Austrian Coffee Cake

1¼ cups raisins, 6 tablespoons rum or orange juice,
4 cups all-purpose flour, 1 package (¼ ounce) active
dry yeast, ½ cup sugar, 1 pinch salt, 1 cup (2 sticks)
softened butter, ½ cup lukewarm milk (110–120°F),
4 eggs, ¾ cup coarsely chopped, Blanched almonds
Plus: Softened butter, A little flour for the pan,
Powdered sugar for garnish

Grease a bundt pan and dust with flour. Rinse raisins in hot water, dry and marinate in rum or orange juice.

In a large bowl of an electric mixer, combine flour, yeast, sugar and salt. Add butter, milk and eggs. Using dough hook attachment on the highest speed, knead mixture into a soft dough. Cover and let stand in a warm place for at least 1 hour.

Knead marinated raisins and almonds into the dough. Transfer to the prepared bundt pan, cover and let rise in a warm place for 30–40 minutes.

Preheat oven to 350°F. Bake cake for about 1 hour. Leave in the pan for several minutes, then invert onto a cooling rack and dust with powdered sugar.

Linzer Torte

Makes 1 springform pan (10 inches diameter)

1 cup blanched, ground almonds, 1¼ cups flour,
3 egg yolks, ¾ cup (1½ sticks) cold butter, cut
into pieces, Juice and peel from ½ lemon, 1 pinch
each of sugar, Salt, Cloves and cinnamon,
¾ cup raspberry jam or currant jelly
Plus: Butter for the pan, Flour for the work surface

Combine almonds and flour. Quickly knead together
with 2 of the egg yolks, butter, lemon juice, lemon
zest, sugar, salt and spices. Shape into a ball, wrap in
plastic wrap and refrigerate for 2 hours.

Preheat oven to 400°F. Grease the bottom of the
springform pan. Place two-thirds of the dough
between 2 sheets of plastic wrap and, on a floured
work surface, roll out to an 11 inch disk. Remove top
sheet of plastic wrap, place the dough in the pan with
the uncovered side down and remove the other sheet
of plastic wrap. Tuck edges of dough into the pan and
spread with jam or jelly. Roll out remaining dough, cut
into narrow strips using a pastry wheel or knife, and
arrange in a lattice pattern on top of the jam.

Whisk together the third egg yolk and several drops of
water and brush onto the dough lattice and edges.
Bake in the oven for 40 minutes.

Nut Torte

For the dough: 1½ cups all-purpose flour,
¾ cup cold butter, cut into pieces,
6 tablespoons sugar, 1 pinch salt, 1 egg
For the filling: 2 tablespoons butter, 1 cup sugar,
3 tablespoons honey, 1 cup cream,
2½ cups coarsely chopped walnuts
Plus: 1 egg yolk for brushing on

Dough: Knead together all the ingredients. Shape into a ball, wrap in plastic wrap and refrigerate for 30 minutes.

Filling: In a saucepan, melt butter, sugar and caramelize over medium heat until golden-brown. Add honey and slowly add cream. Stir in nuts, bring to a boil and let cool.

Preheat oven to 400°F. Grease springform pan (9–10 inch diameter). Roll out a little more than half of the dough between 2 sheets of plastic wrap to a disk with a diameter of about 12 inches. Remove plastic wrap and place dough in the pan, forming a border 2 inches high on the sides. Spread nut mixture onto the dough and fold in the extra dough around the edges.

Roll out remaining dough to a 9½ inch disk. Spread whisked egg yolk onto the dough edges folded over the nut mixture. Place the dough disk on top and press together around the edges. Spread dough with whisked egg yolk and prick with a fork into a wavy pattern. Bake for 40 minutes until golden.

French Apple Tart

Makes 1 tart pan (9–10 inches diameter)

For the dough: ½ cup all-purpose flour, 1 egg yolk,
3 tablespoons cold butter, cut into pieces,
¼ cup powdered sugar
For the filling: 3 small tart apples (Granny Smith),
2 tablespoons lemon juice, 3 tablespoons butter,
1 tablespoon sugar, 3 tablespoons pine nuts
Plus: Butter for the pan

Dough: Quickly knead together ingredients for the dough, if necessary adding several drops of cold water. Shape into a ball, wrap in plastic wrap and refrigerate for 2 hours.

Preheat oven to 350°F. Grease the bottom of the tart pan. Place dough between 2 sheets of plastic wrap and roll out to a thin disk. Remove plastic and place dough in the pan, forming a narrow border around the edges. Pierce dough with a fork. Bake for 15 minutes until golden.

Filling: Cut apples into quarters, peel and remove cores. Cut into wedges and drizzle with lemon juice. In a saucepan, melt butter.

Remove crust from the oven. Pierce any bubbles that formed in the crust. Arrange apple wedges on crust in a starburst pattern, sprinkle with sugar and pine nuts. Drizzle butter and bake 30 more minutes. Serve warm.

Apple Strudel

For the dough: 2 cups all-purpose flour, 1 egg, 1 pinch
salt, 2 tablespoons oil, ½ cup lukewarm water
For the filling: 3½ pounds apples, Juice from 1–2
lemons, 1 teaspoon vanilla extract, 8 ounces Amaretti
cookies or ladyfingers, ½ cup (1 stick) melted butter,
6 tablespoons sugar, ¾ cup pine nuts or slivered
almonds, 1 teaspoon cinnamon
Plus: Flour for the work surface, Butter for the baking
sheet (optional), Powdered sugar for garnish

Knead flour, egg, salt, oil and water to form a smooth,
elastic strudel dough. Add several drops of water or a
little flour so that the dough is not sticky. Shape into a
ball, wrap in plastic wrap and refrigerate for 30 minutes.

Filling: Cut apples into quarters, peel, remove cores,
cut into thin wedges and immediately dredge in lemon
juice. Crumble Amaretti or ladyfingers.

Preheat oven to 375°F. Roll out dough on a very lightly
floured surface. Transfer to a lightly floured kitchen
towel and stretch by hand until paper thin. Brush with
half the melted butter and sprinkle with Amaretti or
ladyfinger crumbs.

Drain apples and toss with vanilla; distribute evenly on
the dough. Combine sugar, pine nuts, almonds, and
cinnamon and sprinkle over the top. With the aid of
the kitchen towel, roll up the dough while folding in

the two sides. Transfer the cylinder to a baking sheet lined with parchment paper or greased with butter and brush with remaining melted butter. Bake in the oven for about 45 minutes until golden. Remove, dust with powdered sugar and serve with vanilla ice cream or vanilla sauce.

Sachertorte

Originating in Vienna, Sachertorte has spread throughout the entire world. Today, this simple yet sophisticated chocolate torte is still being shipped from the famous Sacher Hotel to destinations all over the globe. In 1832, an apprentice chef with the now famous name Sacher created this masterpiece for Prince Metternich. As a reward, he was promoted to head chef. He later bequeathed the recipe to his son Eduard, the hotel's founder.

Makes 1 springform pan (10 inches diameter)

12 ounces semisweet or bittersweet chocolate, divided,
6 eggs, 14 tablespoons softened butter,
$1\frac{1}{2}$ cups powdered sugar, $1\frac{1}{4}$ cups all-purpose flour,
$3\frac{1}{4}$ cup ground almonds, 1 tablespoon cocoa powder,
$3\frac{1}{4}$ cup apricot jam
Plus: Butter and flour for the pan

Preheat oven to 350°F. Grease springform pan thoroughly and dust with flour. Coarsely chop 4 ounces chocolate, melt in a double boiler and let cool slightly.

Separate eggs. Beat egg whites until stiff and refrigerate. Beat egg yolks, butter and powdered sugar until thick and creamy. Gradually stir melted, slightly cooled chocolate into the egg yolk mixture. Combine flour, almonds and cocoa powder; fold into the batter. Then spoon egg whites on top and fold in carefully. Immediately transfer batter to the prepared pan and bake in the oven for about 50 minutes. When done, remove from the oven and let cool slightly. Then remove from the pan and let cool on a cooling rack.

In a small saucepan, heat jam and brush onto cake on all sides. Let cool. Finally, chop remaining chocolate and melt in a warm double boiler. Let stand while stirring occasionally until chocolate has almost hardened and then melt again in the double boiler over low heat (this "tempers" the chocolate so that it later becomes nice and glossy). Pour onto the cake and use a warm spatula to spread chocolate evenly, including down the sides. Then use the spatula to score the surface of the chocolate where you will be cutting it into pieces, making the cake easier to cut later on. Let stand until chocolate is hardened.

Black Forest Cherry Cake

Makes 1 springform pan (10–11 inches diameter)

For the batter: 4 eggs, 1 cup sugar, 4–5 tablespoons
lukewarm water, 5 tablespoons all-purpose flour,
5 tablespoons cocoa powder,
1 teaspoon baking powder, 8 tablespoons cornstarch
For the filling: 1 jar (26 ounces) unsweetened, pitted
sour cherries, 2 tablespoons sugar, 1 cinnamon stick,
$^1/_4$ cup cherry brandy, 2$^1/_2$ cups cream, $^1/_4$ cup sugar,
1 teaspoon vanilla extract, 2 ounce piece of
semisweet or bittersweet chocolate

Batter: Preheat oven to 375°F. Line the bottom of a
springform pan with parchment paper. Separate eggs.
Beat egg whites until stiff while gradually sprinkling in
half the sugar. Beat egg yolks, remaining sugar and
lukewarm water until very foamy. Spoon egg whites on
top of the egg yolk mixture. Combine flour, cocoa powder, baking powder and 5 tablespoons cornstarch,
sprinkle onto egg whites and stir gently using a wire
whisk. Transfer immediately to the prepared pan and
smooth out the surface. Bake on the middle rack for 30
minutes. Then invert onto a cooling rack and let cool.

Cut horizontally into three layers as follows: Lightly
score the cake twice all around the outside. Insert a
long thread into each marking, cross the thread ends
in front and pull through the cake. Repeat to make
three layers.

Filling: Drain cherries well, saving the juice. In a small saucepan, combine cherry juice and enough water if needed to make $3/4$ cup, 2 tablespoons sugar and cinnamon stick; bring to a boil. Stir remaining 3 tablespoons cornstarch into a little water until smooth; gradually stir into cherry juice, using just enough to thicken juice. Boil briefly. Set aside several cherries for garnish and stir remaining cherries into thickened cherry juice. Let cool slightly and remove cinnamon stick.

Combine cherry brandy and a little cherry juice from the jar and drizzle onto the cake layers. Place the bottom layer on a cake plate and fasten a tart ring or the ring from the springform pan around the outside of the cake. Spoon on half of the cherry compote and let cool.

Beat cream, sugar and vanilla until stiff. Spread a little whipped cream onto the cherries and place the second layer on top. Spread on remaining cherries, more cream and top with the last layer. Remove the tart ring and spread cream on all sides of the cake. Grate chocolate coarsely or shave using a vegetable peeler. Garnish cake as desired with grated chocolate or chocolate shavings and with reserved cherries.

⬤ You can bake the chocolate sponge a day ahead of time, but the cake should not be filled and assembled until just before serving.

Cakes & Desserts Made with Coffee

Sponge Omelets with Cappuccino Cream

For the batter: 2 eggs, 6 tablespoons sugar,
2 tablespoons hot water, $\frac{1}{2}$ cup all-purpose flour,
2 tablespoons cornstarch
For the cream: 1 teaspoon plain gelatin ($\frac{1}{2}$ of
.25 ounce package), $\frac{1}{3}$ cup milk, $\frac{1}{4}$ cup espresso,
2 egg yolks, 3 tablespoons sugar,
1 pinch cinnamon, $\frac{1}{2}$ cup cream
Plus: Sugar for garnish

Preheat oven to 350°F. On a sheet of parchment paper, draw 6 circles that are at least 4 inches across and place the paper face down on a baking sheet. For the batter: Separate eggs. Beat egg whites until stiff while sprinkling in half the sugar. Beat egg yolks, remaining sugar and hot water until foamy. Fold in half the egg whites. Place remaining egg whites on top. Combine flour and cornstarch, sprinkle onto egg whites and fold in gently. Spread dough onto the circles you drew and immediately bake in the oven for about 10 minutes.

Sprinkle sponge disks with sugar. Cover with a kitchen towel and turn baking sheet over with the towel in place. Lift off the baking sheet and carefully remove parchment paper. Carefully slit open sponge cakes horizontally with the handle of a wooden spoon and close up again. Let cool on a cooling rack.

For the cream: Soften gelatin in cold water according to package directions. Heat milk and espresso. Beat egg yolks, sugar and cinnamon over a warm double boiler until foamy. Gradually add milk-espresso mixture and beat until it forms a thick cream. Refrigerate cappuccino cream until it starts to gel.

Stir gelatin into the cream. Beat cream until stiff and fold into the cappuccino cream, then refrigerate for 1 hour. Spoon cream into a pastry bag with a large star tip and pipe into the sponge cakes.

Small Espresso Torte

Makes 1 springform pan (6–7 inches diameter)

For the batter: 2 small eggs, 2 tablespoons sugar,
1 tablespoon warm water, 3 tablespoons
ground almonds, 3 tablespoons flour,
2 tablespoons melted butter
For the filling: 1 teaspoon plain gelatin ($\frac{1}{2}$ of
.25 ounce package), 4 tablespoons hot espresso
(or very strong coffee), 8 ounces mascarpone,
2 tablespoons sugar, 2 tablespoons coffee liqueur
Plus: Butter for the pan, Cocoa powder for garnish

Preheat oven to 400°F. Grease bottom of springform
pan. For the batter: Separate eggs. Beat egg yolks, sugar
and warm water until creamy. Beat egg whites until stiff
and spoon onto egg yolk mixture. Combine almonds
and flour and sprinkle on top. Gently mix all these ingredients together. Finally, quickly stir in melted butter.

Transfer batter to the prepared pan and bake in the
oven for about 15 minutes until golden. Leave in the
pan and cool on a rack.

For the filling: Soften gelatin in cold water according to
package directions. Add to hot espresso, then stir in
mascarpone and sugar. Refrigerate mixture for about
30 minutes until it starts to gel.

Remove sponge from the pan and cut in half horizontally. Drizzle layers with coffee liqueur and reassemble with a little coffee cream in between. Spread cream onto the top and sides and dust with a thin coating of cocoa powder.

Coffee Crumb Cake

Makes 1 springform pan (9 inches diameter)

For the batter: $^3/_4$ cup plus 2 tablespoons milk,
1 tablespoon ground coffee, $^1/_4$ cup softened butter,
2 eggs, $^1/_2$ cup sugar, 2 cups all-purpose flour,
2 teaspoons baking powder, 1 pinch salt
For the streusel: $^1/_2$ cup walnuts, 7 tablespoons flour,
6 tablespoons brown sugar, 3 tablespoons
softened butter, $^1/_2$ teaspoon cinnamon
Plus: Butter for the pan

For the batter: Bring milk to a boil. Stir in ground coffee and let cool. Preheat oven to 350°F. Grease springform thoroughly. Beat butter, eggs and sugar until creamy. Combine flour, baking powder and salt, then stir flour mixture and coffee milk into the egg mixture. Spoon batter into the springform pan and smooth out the surface.

For the streusel: Chop walnuts finely and combine with flour, sugar, butter and cinnamon. Sprinkle over the cake and bake for about 35 minutes until golden-brown.

Little Pear Coffee Cake

Makes 1 small bundt pan (about 4 cups volume)

²/₃ cup softened butter, 6 tablespoons sugar, 3 eggs,
1 cup all-purpose flour, ¹/₂ cup plus 1 tablespoon
cornstarch, 3 tablespoons instant coffee,
2 tablespoons cocoa powder, 1 tablespoon baking
powder, 1 pear, 2 tablespoons lemon juice,
4 ounces semisweet chocolate
Plus: Butter for the pan

Preheat oven to 400°F. Carefully grease bundt pan.
Beat butter and sugar until creamy and stir in eggs one
at a time. Combine flour, cornstarch, 2 tablespoons
instant coffee, cocoa powder and baking powder, and
stir this mixture into the batter.

Peel pear, cut into quarters, remove core, dice finely,
drizzle with lemon juice and stir into batter. Spoon batter into prepared pan, smooth out the surface and
bake in the oven for about 45 minutes.

In a small bowl, heat chocolate in the microwave on
high 1–2 minutes until melted. Stir in remaining
1 tablespoon of instant coffee. Let cool slightly and
drizzle over cake as desired.

Espresso Almond Waffles

5 tablespoons softened butter, 2 eggs, 2 tablespoons
sugar, 3/4 cup plus 1 tablespoon all-purpose flour,
1 teaspoon baking powder, 1/4 cup cream,
1/4 cup cold espresso (or very strong coffee),
1/4 cup sliced almonds
Plus: Grease for the waffle iron,
Powdered sugar for garnish

Beat butter, eggs and sugar until nice and creamy.
Combine flour and baking powder. Stir flour mixture,
cream and coffee into the batter. Finally, fold in
almonds.

Heat and grease waffle iron. Spoon in one-quarter of
the batter and smooth the surface slightly. Close waffle iron and cook batter until golden. One-by-one, prepare another 3 waffles. Dust with powdered sugar and
serve immediately while still warm.

🍴 Serve with whipped cream mixed with grated
chocolate and a little coffee liqueur. Or mix mascarpone, sugar, lemon juice and lemon zest until
creamy and serve on the side.

Espresso Zabaglione with Oranges

For the zabaglione: 2 egg yolks, 6 tablespoons sugar,
$\frac{1}{4}$ cup strong espresso, $\frac{1}{2}$ cup cream, 2 tablespoons
cream sherry, 2 oranges, 1 teaspoon butter,
1 tablespoon maple syrup

For the zabaglione: In a bowl, beat egg yolks and sugar until foamy. Add espresso and beat over a warm double boiler until frothy. Remove from double boiler and stir until cooled (the best way is to set it on a bowl of ice cubes). Beat cream until stiff and fold into cold espresso cream. Flavor with sherry and refrigerate until serving.

Section the oranges, saving any juice they produce. In a small nonstick pan, heat butter and maple syrup and stir in orange sections. Add orange juice and distribute on dessert plates. Top with zabaglione.

Mousse au Café

4 ounces semisweet chocolate or chocolate chips,
2 tablespoons very strong coffee, 2 eggs,
3 tablespoons sugar, 2 tablespoons hot water,
$\frac{1}{2}$ cup cream, 1 teaspoon cocoa powder,
1 tablespoon grated chocolate

Combine chocolate and coffee in a microwave safe dish. Heat on high power 1–2 minutes, stirring until chocolate is melted. Cool slightly.

Separate eggs. Using an electric mixer, beat egg yolks, sugar and hot water until creamy. Fold in melted chocolate. Beat egg whites and cream separately until stiff and gradually fold each into the egg yolk mixture.

Transfer to a bowl, cover and refrigerate for at least 2 hours. To serve, scoop mousse onto plates and sprinkle with cocoa and grated chocolate.

Tiramisu

2 egg yolks, 2 tablespoons sugar,
4 tablespoons hot water, 8 ounces mascarpone ,
1 teaspoon lemon zest lemon,
$\frac{1}{3}$ cup espresso (or very strong coffee),
5 tablespoons amaretto, brandy and/or coffee liqueur,
3–4 ounces ladyfingers, Cocoa powder

In a bowl, beat egg yolks, sugar and hot water for about 5 minutes until thick and creamy. Stir in mascarpone one spoonful at a time, followed by the lemon zest.

Combine espresso and amaretto, brandy and/or coffee liqueur. Briefly dunk half the ladyfingers in the espresso and arrange on the bottom of a shallow dish.

Spread half the cream on top. Briefly dip remaining ladyfingers in espresso and arrange on top. Spread with remaining cream. Cover and refrigerate for at least 3 hours. Before serving, dust with a thick layer of cocoa powder.

Tuscan Coffee Flan

1 3/4 cups milk, 2 eggs, 4 egg yolks, 1/2 cup sugar,
1/2 cup strong, hot espresso, Powdered sugar and
cocoa powder for garnish

Preheat oven to 300°F. Bring milk to a boil; set aside.
Using the whisk attachment on an electric mixer, beat
eggs, egg yolks and sugar until creamy. Gradually add
espresso and hot milk while mixing gently, not letting
the mixture become too foamy. Pour cream into an
ovenproof bowl. Set this bowl inside a slightly larger
ovenproof bowl and fill the larger bowl with hot water
up to the same level as the egg cream in the smaller
bowl. Bake in the oven for about 60 minutes until firm.
Invert onto a plate, dust with powdered sugar and
cocoa powder, before serving.

Coffee Chocolate Soufflé

3 ounces semisweet chocolate, 2 tablespoons
instant coffee, Several drops hot water, 3 eggs,
1 tablespoon warm water, 1 tablespoon sugar,
½ teaspoon vanilla, 1 tablespoon flour
Plus: Grease for the ramekins,
Powdered sugar for garnish

Preheat oven to 350°F. Thoroughly grease four ½-cup
size ramekins. Chop chocolate coarsely and melt in a
warm double boiler. Dissolve coffee in a little hot water
and stir into chocolate.

Separate eggs. Beat egg whites until stiff and set aside.
Beat egg yolks, warm water, sugar and vanilla until
creamy. Stir in melted chocolate. Fold in half the egg
whites and spoon the rest on top. Sprinkle with flour
and fold in carefully.

Spoon batter into prepared ramekins and bake in the
oven for about 25 minutes. Dust with powdered sugar
and serve immediately.

🍴 Serve with a creamy vanilla sauce or vanilla ice
cream stirred until smooth.

Mocha Truffles

6 ounces semisweet chocolate or chocolate chips,
$\frac{1}{2}$ cup cream, 4 tablespoons very strong espresso,
$\frac{1}{2}$ cup softened butter,
5–6 tablespoons cocoa powder

Chop chocolate and place in a small saucepan along with cream. Melt over low heat while stirring constantly. Remove from heat, stir in espresso and let cool. Beat butter until creamy and gradually fold in the chocolate mixture. Cover and refrigerate for at least 2 hours.

One teaspoonful at a time, quickly roll chocolate mixture between your hands to form balls, repeatedly chilling your hands under cold water. Immediately roll the balls in cocoa powder, place in small paper candy cups and keep in a cool place.

❶ Always store truffles in a cool place so they won't become too soft. Alternatively, don't roll balls in cocoa powder after shaping; instead, dip in melted coating chocolate (that is no longer hot). Once they cool, the soft truffle balls will be protected in a solid chocolate coating.

Espresso Cappuccino Gelatin

For the gelatin: 1 package (.25 ounces) plain gelatin, divided, 1 cup strong, hot espresso, 3 tablespoons powdered sugar, 3/4 cup plus 2 tablespoons cream
For the sauce: 1/2 cup cream, 2 tablespoons powdered sugar, 4 tablespoons amaretto

For the gelatin: In 2 separate bowls, soften 1/2 teaspoon gelatin and remaining gelatin in enough cold water to soften. Whisk together espresso and powdered sugar. Measure out 2/3 cup of the espresso and dissolve 1/2 teaspoon of gelatin in this espresso.

Dissolve the rest of the gelatin in the remaining espresso, add cream and stir until slightly foamy. In tall glasses, alternate layers of the 2 espresso mixtures, letting each layer gel before adding the next. Finish with a dark espresso layer.

For the sauce: Beat cream until softly whipped; stir in powdered sugar and amaretto, and use as a topping for the desserts.

Espresso Parfait

1 cup cream, 4 egg yolks, $\frac{1}{2}$ cup powdered sugar,
$\frac{1}{4}$ cup warm water, $\frac{1}{4}$ cup strong, hot espresso
$1\frac{1}{4}$ cups raisins, $\frac{1}{2}$ cup dry sherry,
1 tablespoon lemon juice

Beat cream until stiff and then refrigerate. Beat egg yolks, powdered sugar and warm water until frothy. Stir in espresso and then fold in cream.

Spoon mixture into a freezer-safe bowl and freeze for at least 3 hours.

Rinse raisins under hot water and drain well. In a bowl, combine raisins, sherry and lemon juice, cover and marinate.

Remove parfait from freezer about 15 minutes before serving. Top with marinated raisins.

Granita di Caffè

1 cup strong, hot espresso, 6 tablespoons sugar,
1 pinch ground vanilla, 1 teaspoon cocoa powder

Combine hot espresso, sugar, vanilla and cocoa powder. Let cool. Pour into a freezer-safe bowl, cover and freeze for about 4 hours, occasionally removing from the freezer and stirring vigorously. To serve, separate ice into pieces with a fork.

Favorite Snacks in Espresso Bars & Coffee Shops

Olive Ciabatta with Mortadella

3½ ounces provolone cheese, thinly sliced,
Several leaves oakleaf lettuce, 1 red bell pepper,
1 onion, 1 loaf ciabatta bread with olives,
¼ cup softened butter, Freshly ground black pepper,
3½ ounces mortadella, thinly sliced

Clean oakleaf lettuce, rinse, pat dry and, if desired, tear into bite-sized pieces. Cut bell pepper in half, remove stem, seeds and interior, and cut into narrow strips. Peel onion, slice thinly and separate slices into rings.

Cut ciabatta in half horizontally and spread both halves with butter. Distribute provolone on the bottom half and season with pepper. Top with lettuce leaves, bell pepper strips, onion rings and mortadella. Cover with top half of ciabatta and press together firmly. Cut finished ciabatta into 4 pieces.

Panini with Taleggio

2 firm tomatoes, 4 ciabatta rolls,
A little softened butter, 3 ounces thinly sliced Taleggio
(semi-hard Italian cheese), Several basil leaves,
4 slices Coppa (special Italian sausage) or Parma ham,
Coarsely ground black pepper

Remove cores from tomatoes and slice. Cut ciabatta
rolls in half and spread with a thin layer of softened
butter. Top bottom halves with cheese slices, basil,
Coppa or Parma ham, and tomatoes. Season with
coarsely ground black pepper and replace the top
halves. Press together lightly.

Tramezzini with Gorgonzola

6 dried tomatoes in oil, patted dry,
2 ounces mascarpone, 3 ounces Gorgonzola,
2 cloves garlic, Salt, Freshly ground black pepper,
Several leaves radicchio, 8 slices white bread,
3 ounces pastrami or corned beef, thinly sliced

Dice tomatoes very finely and mix with mascarpone
and Gorgonzola. Peel garlic, squeeze through a press
and add to mixture. Season with salt and pepper.

Rinse radicchio, pat thoroughly dry and cut into strips.
Remove crusts from bread and spread with the Gorgonzola cream. Top 4 bread slices with radicchio, then

pastrami or corned beef, and finally the other bread slices with the Gorgonzola cream side down. Press together firmly and cut in half diagonally.

Focaccia with Mozzarella, Parmesan and Tomatoes

1 pound refrigerated or frozen thawed pizza dough,
A little flour for handling the dough, 4½ ounces
mozzarella cheese, 2½ ounces grated Parmesan,
2 small, firm tomatoes, 2 cloves garlic,
4 tablespoons olive oil, 2 teaspoons dried oregano,
Salt, Freshly ground black pepper

Preheat oven to 425°F. Dust your hands with flour and on a baking sheet lined with parchment paper, shape pizza dough into a large oval about 8 x 12 inches. Slice mozzarella thinly. Remove cores from tomatoes and slice.

Peel garlic, squeeze through a press and place in a cup with olive oil. Stir and drizzle evenly on the dough. Top with mozzarella, Parmesan and tomatoes. Season with oregano, salt and pepper. Bake in the oven on the bottom rack for 20–25 minutes until golden-brown.

Red Onion Quiche with Pine Nuts

1¼ pounds red onions, Several sprigs thyme,
1 tablespoon oil, 3½ ounces smoked bacon, diced,
1 clove garlic, Salt, Freshly ground black pepper,
1 sheet readymade puff pastry, 1 cup cream,
3 eggs, 3½ ounces grated Swiss cheese,
3 tablespoons pine nuts
Plus: Flour for the work surface

Peel onions, slice thinly and separate into rings. Rinse thyme, pat dry and remove leaves from stems.

In a pan, heat oil and fry bacon until crispy. Add onions and cook until softened. Peel garlic, squeeze through a press and add. Season with thyme, salt and pepper and cook over low heat for 10 minutes.

Preheat oven to 400°F. Roll out puff pastry dough. Rinse out a 10½ inch quiche pan with cold water, line with pastry and trim excess from around the edges. Pierce bottom of crust several times with a fork.

Distribute onion mixture on puff pastry. Whisk cream and eggs and pour over the mixture. Sprinkle with cheese and pine nuts. Bake in the oven for about 30 minutes.

Double Cheeseburger

2 pounds beef (e.g. shoulder or flank), Salt,
Freshly ground pepper, Oil for frying (optional),
8 small slices tangy cheese (e.g. Gruyère or Cheddar),
2 red onions, 8 lettuce leaves, 1 cucumber,
4 large, firm tomatoes, 6 hamburger rolls,
4 tablespoons medium-hot mustard,
4 tablespoons ketchup, 4 tablespoons chili sauce

Remove sinews and some (but not all) of the excess
fat from beef. Grind beef in a meat grinder, but not
too finely (otherwise hamburgers will be dry), and
season with salt and pepper. Shape into 8 round
patties about 1 inch thick and even out the edges
(don't knead too much!).

Fry patties on a tabletop grill or in a pan with oil for
3–4 minutes on each side. In the last few minutes, top
with cheese and let it melt slightly.

Peel onion and slice thinly. Clean lettuce leaves, rinse
and pat thoroughly dry. Peel cucumber and slice.
Remove cores from tomatoes and slice. Cut hamburger
rolls in half and toast lightly (each burger requires
3 roll halves). Spread each half with mustard, ketchup
and chili sauce. Stack all the ingredients as desired to
make 4 double cheeseburgers and gently press together.

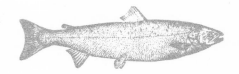

Bagels with Cream Cheese and Lox

For the dough: 1 cup milk, $^1/_4$ cup butter, 1 tablespoon
sugar, $^1/_2$ teaspoon salt, 1 package active dry yeast,
1 egg white, About 2 cups all-purpose flour
For the topping: 14 ounces cream cheese, Salt,
Freshly ground black pepper,
7–8 ounces smoked salmon, thinly sliced
Plus: Flour for the work surface,
1 egg yolk for brushing on

For the dough: In a saucepan, heat milk, butter, sugar
and salt while stirring until the butter has melted.
Transfer to a bowl and let cool until lukewarm. Stir in
yeast and let dissolve. Let stand for 10 minutes until
foamy.

In a cup, whisk egg white and beat into the yeast mixture. Gradually add flour and knead to form a smooth,
very soft dough. Knead for 10 minutes, cover and let
rise in a warm place for about 1 hour.

Divide dough into 12–16 pieces and shape into balls. Punch a hole through the center of each ball with your index finger. On a lightly floured surface, work your finger around inside each ring until the hole diameter reaches about 1 inch. Cover the rings and let rise for about 10 more minutes.

In a pot, bring a large amount of water to a boil. Add 3–4 dough rings at a time and precook for no more than 1 minute. Remove with a slotted spoon, drain well and place on 2 baking sheets lined with parchment paper.

Preheat oven to 400°F. Whisk together egg yolk and 1 tablespoon water and brush onto bagels. Bake in the oven for 15–20 minutes until golden-brown.

Before serving, cut bagels in half, toast if desired. For the topping: Spread bottom halves with cream cheese, season with salt and pepper and top with salmon. Then cover with the top halves.

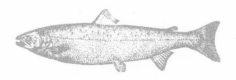

BLT

This is one of the greatest classics among American sandwiches

>   7 ounces sliced bacon, 4 large lettuce leaves,
> 2 large, firm tomatoes, 8 slices sandwich bread,
> 5–6 tablespoons aioli (garlic flavored mayonnaise) or
> mayonnaise, Salt, Freshly ground black pepper

In a large pan, fry bacon over medium heat until crispy. Drain on paper towels and let cool.

Clean lettuce leaves, rinse and pat thoroughly dry. Remove cores from tomatoes and slice.

Toast bread and spread with aioli or mayonnaise. Top 4 slices with remaining ingredients, seasoning tomato slices with salt and pepper. Place remaining bread slices on top and cut sandwiches in half diagonally.

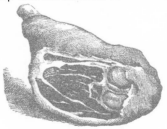

Turkey Salad Sandwich

2 small turkey cutlets, Salt, Freshly ground black
pepper, 2 tablespoons oil, 1 onion, 2 stalks celery,
1 cup canned corn, drained, 2 tablespoons capers,
6 tablespoons mayonnaise, 2 tablespoons yogurt,
8 slices sandwich bread,
4 tablespoons softened butter, 8 lettuce leaves

Rinse cutlets under cold water and pat dry. Rub with
salt and pepper. In a pan, heat oil and sear meat on all
sides. Then sauté on both sides over medium heat for
about 2 minutes.

In the meantime, peel onion and dice finely. Clean
celery and slice thinly.

Dice turkey finely. In a bowl, combine turkey, onion,
celery, corn and capers. Carefully stir in mayonnaise
and yogurt. Season with salt and pepper, cover and let
stand for about 30 minutes.

To serve, toast bread and spread with butter. Clean
lettuce leaves, rinse, pat dry and place on bread slices.
Distribute turkey salad on 4 of the slices and place the
other slices on top with the lettuce side down. Press
together lightly and cut in half either lengthwise or
diagonally. Secure with toothpicks.

Tuna Sandwich

2 tablespoons aioli (garlic flavored mayonnaise),
4 tablespoons yogurt, Several leaves fresh marjoram,
Salt, Freshly ground black pepper,
A little zest from a lemon,
1 can (6 ounces) tuna in water, 2 dried tomatoes
in oil, patted dry, 3 1/2 ounces feta, crumbled,
20 pitted green olives, 1 cucumber, 8 slices rye bread

Combine aioli, yogurt and marjoram and season with salt, pepper and lemon zest. Drain tuna. Cut tomatoes into fine strips. Slice olives. In a bowl, combine tuna, tomatoes, feta and olives. Peel cucumber and slice.

Spread bread with aioli-yogurt sauce and top 4 slices with sliced cucumber. Spread with tuna mixture. Place remaining bread slices on top with the spread side down and press together lightly. Toast in a sandwich toaster for about 5 minutes.

Egg Salad Sandwich

4 eggs, 1 red bell pepper, 4 stalks celery,
4 tablespoons mayonnaise, 4 tablespoons yogurt,
2 tablespoons lemon juice, Salt, Freshly ground
black pepper, ½ teaspoon curry, 4 baguette rolls,
4 tablespoons softened butter, 4 lettuce leaves

Boil eggs for about 8 minutes. Rinse under cold water,
peel and dice. Cut bell pepper in half, remove stem,
seeds and interior, and dice finely. Clean celery and
dice finely.

Combine mayonnaise and yogurt and season with
lemon juice, salt, pepper and curry. Mix with vegeta-
bles. Carefully fold in diced eggs. Cut rolls in half and
spread with butter. Clean lettuce leaves, rinse, pat dry
and place on bottom halves of rolls. Top with egg
salad, cover with top roll halves and press together
lightly.

Roast Beef Sandwich Rolls

$1/2$ cup walnuts, 7 ounces cream cheese, Salt,
Freshly ground black pepper, 3 ounces arugula leaves,
4 thin slices white bread (loaf of bread
sliced horizontally), 8 tablespoons softened butter,
16 thin slices roast beef

Finely chop walnuts and mix with cream cheese.
Season with salt and pepper. Rinse arugula, pat thoroughly dry and remove coarse stems. Remove crust
from bread and butter lightly. Spread with walnut-cheese spread and top with arugula and roast beef.

Starting from a narrower end, roll up bread slices,
wrap tightly in aluminum foil and refrigerate for about
1 hour. Then slice each roll on an angle.

❶ This works only with extremely fresh and very thinly
sliced bread. Normal sandwich bread breaks when
you roll it.

Cheese Club Sandwich

16 slices sandwich bread, 6 small, firm tomatoes,
12 large lettuce leaves, 7 ounces cream cheese, Salt,
Freshly ground black pepper, Paprika, 12 tablespoons
softened herb butter, 4 slices Swiss cheese, 4 slices
Cheddar cheese, 5 ounces blue cheese

Toast bread slices. Remove cores from tomatoes and
slice. Clean lettuce leaves, rinse and pat dry. Combine
cream cheese, salt, pepper and paprika.

Spread 4 bread slices with a little herb butter. Top each
with 1 lettuce leaf, 1 slice cheese and about 3 slices
tomato. Spread 4 bread slices with cream cheese and
place on top of the first 4 slices with the spread side
down. Spread the top sides with herb butter and
repeat the entire procedure described above. Finish
the sandwiches by topping them with bread slices
spread with cream cheese, with the spread side down.

Vegetarian Wraps

1 onion, 1 large green bell pepper, 1 tablespoon oil,
1 clove garlic, 1 can (15 ounces) kidney beans,
1 can (6 ounces) tomato paste,
1 teaspoon dried thyme, Salt, Freshly ground pepper,
Cumin, Several drops Tabasco,
4 green or plain tortillas, Several leaves iceberg lettuce,
2 small, firm tomatoes,
Mexican spices, if desired,
$\frac{1}{4}$ cup coarsely grated Emmenthaler or Cheddar,
$\frac{1}{4}$ cup sour cream

Peel onion. Cut bell pepper in half and remove core, seeds and interior. Finely dice onion and pepper and brown lightly in hot oil while stirring. Peel garlic, squeeze through a press and add.

Drain beans in a colander. Mix tomato paste with a little hot water. Add beans and tomato paste to the bell-pepper mixture. Season with thyme, salt, pepper, cumin and Tabasco and simmer uncovered over low heat for about 10 minutes.

In the meantime, heat tortillas in the oven according to package directions. Clean lettuce, rinse, pat dry and cut into thin strips. Remove cores and seeds from tomatoes and dice finely. Combine lettuce and tomatoes and add Mexican spices, if desired.

Shape tortillas into cones. Fold over the pointed end and wrap in a paper napkin. Fill cone with bean mixture, topping with a tablespoon of cheese and dollop of sour cream. Distribute lettuce-tomato mixture on top and serve wraps immediately.

Poppy Seed Omelet Croissants

2 eggs, $1/4$ cup cream, 1 tablespoon poppy seeds,
Salt, Freshly ground black pepper,
2 tablespoons softened butter, 4 croissants,
1 tablespoon prepared pesto, 4 leaves frisée lettuce,
8 thin slices deli turkey breast

Whisk together eggs, cream and poppy seeds and season with salt and pepper. In a small nonstick pan, heat 1 teaspoon butter. Pour in egg mixture, cover and cook over low heat to make a fluffy omelet. Let cool. Cut croissants in half, spread halves with a thin layer of butter and pesto.

Clean lettuce leaves, rinse, pat dry and, if desired, tear into bite-sized pieces. Place on the bottom croissant halves. Top with turkey breast. Cut omelet into 4 triangles and place on top of turkey. Cover with top croissant halves and press together lightly.

Traditional & New Coffee Drinks

Irish Coffee

4 teaspoons brown sugar, 16 tablespoons Irish
whiskey, 4 cups strong, hot coffee,
Cream whipped until semi-stiff, as desired,
Grated chocolate, as desired

Rinse out 4 Irish coffee mugs with hot water. Place
1/2 teaspoon brown sugar in each cup. Distribute
whiskey in the cups and flambé. Let burn for 1–2 minutes and then add hot coffee. Carefully spoon a little
whipped cream on top but don't let it mix with the
coffee. Sprinkle with grated chocolate. Do not stir.
You should be able to drink the coffee through the
cool topping.

Rum Coffee

4 teaspoons cocoa powder, 4 teaspoons sugar,
8 tablespoons rum, 4 cups strong, hot coffee,
Whipped cream, as desired

Rinse out 4 heat-proof mugs or cups with hot water.
Place cocoa, sugar and rum in the cups and stir. Add
hot coffee and top with whipped cream.

Cognac Coffee

4 egg yolks, 4 tablespoons sugar,
4 teaspoons cognac,
2 cups strong, hot coffee, 2 cups hot milk,
Whipped cream, as desired

In each of 4 tall, heat-proof glasses, combine 1 egg yolk, 1 tablespoon sugar and 1 teaspoon cognac. Evenly distribute coffee and milk in the glasses. If desired, top with whipped cream.

Café Brûlot

8 tablespoons cognac,
4 whole cloves, 1 cinnamon stick,
A little zest from a lemon and orange,
8 tablespoons sugar, 4 cups strong, hot coffee,
Whipped cream, as desired

In a small saucepan, heat cognac, cloves, cinnamon, lemon and orange zest, and sugar without boiling. Carefully flambé.

Pour hot coffee into cups and carefully add flaming cognac, without the spices. If desired, top with whipped cream and serve immediately.

Espresso Punch

3 cups strong espresso,
$1/2$ cup rum, $1/2$ cup red wine,
3 tablespoons coarse sugar crystals,
$1/2$ teaspoon vanilla, 1 cinnamon stick

In a saucepan, heat without letting it boil the espresso, rum, red wine, sugar, vanilla and cinnamon until the sugar has dissolved. Remove the cinnamon and pour into 4 tall heat-proof glasses.

Coffee Maria Theresia

4 cups strong, hot coffee, Sugar (optional),
$1/2$ cup orange liqueur, Whipped cream, as desired,
Multicolored sprinkles

Sweeten coffee with sugar if desired and add orange liqueur. Top with a thick layer of whipped cream and multicolored sprinkles.

Soul Warmer

3¹/₂ ounces semisweet chocolate,
2 cups strong, hot coffee, Cream, as desired,
Cinnamon, Cloves, Freshly grated nutmeg,
Coarse sugar crystals

Chop chocolate. In a small saucepan, melt chocolate in 1 cup water over low heat. Pour into 4 heat-proof glasses and add coffee. Pour in a little cream and season each cup to taste with 1 pinch cinnamon, cloves, nutmeg and a little coarse sugar.

Mocha Flip

2 egg yolks, ¹/₄ cup powdered sugar,
¹/₂ teaspoon vanilla, 1 teaspoon cocoa powder,
1 cup strong, hot espresso

In a bowl over a warm double boiler, beat egg yolks, powdered sugar and vanilla until creamy. Beat in cocoa and then gradually beat in hot espresso. Let stand briefly until some of the foam has disappeared, then pour into glasses or cups and serve immediately.

Advocaat Coffee

2 cups strong, hot coffee, $\frac{1}{2}$ cup advocaat,
$\frac{1}{4}$ cup powdered sugar, 2 tablespoons rum,
Whipped cream, as desired

Combine hot coffee, advocaat, powdered sugar and rum. Pour into cups or glasses and top with a little whipped cream.

Coffee Punch with Sherry

2 cups strong coffee, 4 tablespoons cream sherry,
3 tablespoons sugar, 2 tablespoons rum,
Grated zest from 1 orange, 1 cinnamon stick,
Whipped cream, as desired

Combine coffee, sherry, rum, sugar, orange zest and cinnamon and heat without boiling. Strain into tall glasses and top with a little whipped cream.

Orange Coffee

1 orange, 4 tablespoons orange liqueur,
4–8 teaspoons powdered sugar,
4 cups strong, hot coffee,
Whipped cream, as desired

Using a zester, grate fine zest from the orange. Squeeze juice. Pour orange juice and orange liqueur into 4 tall heat-proof glasses. Sweeten with powdered sugar to taste. Pour in hot coffee, top with whipped cream as desired and sprinkle with orange zest.

  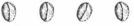

Mazagran

4 cups very strong, hot coffee, Sugar (optional),
Ice cubes, 8 tablespoons maraschino liqueur,
4 dashes Angostura bitters

Sweeten coffee with sugar to taste. Place ice cubes in 4 heat-proof glasses and pour on hot coffee. Divide maraschino and Angostura evenly between glasses. Stir and serve with straws.

Hot-and-Cold Walnut Espresso

4 cups strong, hot espresso, Sugar (optional),
4 scoops walnut ice cream,
Whipped cream, as desired, Walnuts

Sweeten espresso with sugar to taste and pour into 4 tall heat-proof glasses. Add 1 scoop walnut ice cream to each glass. If desired, top with whipped cream and several coarsely chopped walnuts.

Ice Cream Coffee

8 scoops vanilla ice cream,
4 cups strong, ice-cold coffee,
Cream and sugar, as desired,
Cocoa or grated chocolate

Place vanilla ice cream into 4 tall, well-chilled glasses. Pour in strong, ice-cold coffee. Beat cream and sugar until stiff, spoon into a pastry bag and pipe onto the ice cream coffee. Sprinkle with cocoa or grated chocolate and serve with long spoons and straws.

Viennese Iced Coffee

4 cups strong coffee, 8 teaspoons sugar,
³/₄ cup cream

Sweeten coffee with sugar. Stir in cream and refrigerate for several hours. Serve well chilled.

Iced Caffè Amaretto

1 cup strong, cold coffee, 1 cup milk, ¹/₂ cup amaretto
Ice cubes, as desired, Cocoa powder

Combine coffee, milk and amaretto. Place several ice cubes in 4 tall glasses, pour in coffee mixture and sprinkle lightly with cocoa.

Orange Vanilla Coffee

4 cups strong, hot coffee, ¹/₃ cup sugar,
3 oranges, 4 tablespoons orange liqueur,
4 large scoops vanilla ice cream

Sweeten coffee with sugar and chill. Cut thin long spirals of peel from 1 orange and set aside for garnish. Finely dice orange. Squeeze juice from remaining oranges. Place orange flesh and juice in 4 tall glasses, drizzle with orange liqueur, add 1 large scoop ice cream and pour in cold coffee. Garnish with orange peel spirals.

Cold Caribbean Coffee

5–6 ounces fresh pineapple, $\frac{1}{2}$ cup orange juice,
2 tablespoons sugar, 1 cup strong, ice-cold coffee,
4 tablespoons toasted, grated coconut,
$\frac{1}{2}$ cup cream

Cut up pineapple. In a blender, purée pineapple, orange juice and sugar. Gradually blend in coffee. Moisten rims of 4 glasses and dip in grated coconut. Pour coffee into glasses. Whip cream until stiff mix with remaining coconut and spoon over coffee.

Banana Coffee Shake

4 tablespoons instant coffee, 1 large banana,
1 tablespoon lemon juice, 2 tablespoons sugar,
3 cups cold milk

Dissolve coffee in a little hot water. Peel banana and chop coarsely. In a blender, purée banana, lemon juice, sugar and coffee. Gradually blend in milk. Pour into glasses and serve immediately.

List of Recipes

Pastries Typically Served with Coffee

Cakes & Desserts Made with Coffee

Favorite Snacks in Espresso Bars & Coffee Shops

Traditional & New Coffee Drinks